The Finnish Cookbook Traditional and Modern Recipes

Marit Peters

Contents

49 - Ground Meat Soup
50 - Black Pudding With Sour Cream
51 - Stroganoff
52 - Beef and Beetroot Steak
53 - Stuffed Ham
54 - Karelian Stew
55 - Meatballs
56 - Liver Casserole
57 - Chicken in Tomato Sauce
59 - Potato Flat Bread
60 - Semolina Pudding
61 - Barley Bread
62 - Pancakes
63 - Bilberry Tart
64 - Baked Pancake
65 - Cinnamon Rolls
67 - Blueberry Pie
68 - Runeberg Torte
69 - Doughnuts
70 - Fruit Soup
71 - Rice Tarts
73 - Rye Bread
74 - Blueberry and Wild Strawberry Cake
75 - Rye Pudding
76 - Long Drink
77 - Blueberry Milk
78 - Sima
79 - Mulled Wine

Introduction

Finnish food is influenced by its geographical position. It is next to Sweden and Russia and Finnish food shares similarities with those cuisines.

Finnish food has also been influenced by Finland's harsh northern European climate where items were not able to be grown and those that were for a short time. This meany only a limited range of foods were available.

Traditional Finnish foods are woodland berries such as lingonberries, cloudberries, wild strawberries and blueberries. Fish such as salmon and herring. Oats are a staple with porridge being a very popular dish in Finland. Rye is used in Finland to make traditional rye bread and crackers.

It has been said of Finnish food that it is simple and has an emphasis is on fresh ingredients. Today foods from other world cuisines are naturally eaten in Finland but the traditional Finnish simple cooking using high quality fresh ingredients is a big part of Finnish cuisine today.

Try some traditional and contemporary Finnish dishes in this book.

Spinach Soup

Ingredients

220g/7.7 oz of chopped spinach
4 tablespoons of wholemeal flour
4 sliced hard boiled eggs
1 litre/4 cups of milk
60g/2.11 oz of butter
salt
sugar
white pepper

Melt the butter in a saucepan. Mix in the flour to make a paste. Add the milk stirring all the time. Add the spinach. Bring to the boil and cook for two minutes.

Add some salt, sugar and pepper. Garnish with egg.

Mushroom Salad

Ingredients

450g/1 lb of sliced mushrooms
half a grated onion
lettuce
sliced tomato
fresh dill
8 tablespoons of whipping/double cream
65ml/a quarter of cup of sour cream
2 tablespoons of lemon juice
1 teaspoon of sugar
salt
white pepper
black pepper
nutmeg

Mix the mushrooms, sugar, lemon juice, onion, black pepper and white pepper in a bowl.

In another bowl, mix the whipping cream to make a stiff mix. Add the sour cream,, some nutmeg and white pepper and salt. Add to the mushroom mix.

Put lettuce leaves in a bowl. Pour the mushroom mix into them. Add tomato slices and dill on top.

Vegetable Soup

Ingredients

7 peeled potatoes chopped in half
2 peeled and chopped carrots
2 tablespoons of butter
140g/1 cup of green peas
7 baby onions
225g/half a lb of chopped green beans
100g/1 cup of chopped cauliflower
240ml/1 cup of milk
2450ml/1 cup of single/light cream
3 tablespoons of flour
dill
sliced radish
500ml/2 cups of water
a third of a tablespoon of salt
half a teaspoon of pepper

Boil the water in a pan. Add the potatoes, cover, then cook on a low heat for 6 minutes.

Add the onions, beans, cauliflower butter and salt and pepper. Cook on a low heat for 10 minutes.

Add the peas and cook for 3 minutes. Add the flour and mix. Add the cream and milk and stir. Cook on a low heat for 6 minutes.

Garnish with radish and dill before serving.

Sweet Mustard

Ingredients

5 tablespoons of cream
3 tablespoons of sour cream
3 tablespoons of mustard powder
6 tablespoons of sugar
salt
1 tablespoon of honey
1 beaten egg
1 tablespoon of apple cider vinegar

Put the sour cream and cream in a pan. Boil, then put in a bowl. Add the sugar, mustard powder and some salt and mix. Add the honey and mix to make a smooth mix.

Add the egg and mix. Put the mix in a pan and bring to the boil stirring all the time.

Take off the hat and cool. Add the vinegar and mix. Strain the mix then put into a jar and store in the refrigerator.

Will last one week.

Beetroot Salad

Ingredients

4 chopped boiled beetroot
2 chopped boiled potatoes
2 chopped boiled carrots
1 chopped onion
1 chopped apple
2 chopped gherkins
2 teaspoons of cream
2 teaspoons of white vinegar
half a teaspoon if sugar
half a teaspoon of salt

Put the vinegar, salt, cream and sugar in a bowl and mix.

Add the rest of the ingredients and mix.

Rutabaga With Syrup

Ingredients

1 peeled rutabaga cut into cubes
1 tablespoons of syrup
2 and a half tablespoons of butter
salt
pepper

Put the butter and rutabaga in a pan and cook for 7 minutes.
Add the syrup, cover, then cook for 30 minutes on a low heat.

Add salt and pepper.

Sugared Lingonberries

Ingredients

210g/7.4 oz of lingonberries
80g/2.8 oz of caster sugar

Put the sugar and lingonberries in a bowl Mix, for 5 minutes taking care not to crush the berries.

Leave at room temperature for 2 hours.

Put in jars and store in the refrigerator.

Serve with meat.

Carrot Casserole

Ingredients

1 kg/2.3 lb of peeled and sliced carrots
510ml/2 cups of water
1 teaspoon of salt
100g/3.5 oz of rice
200ml/6.7 fl oz of cream
110ml/half a cup of milk
1 egg
salt
3 tablespoons of syrup
nutmeg
pepper
breadcrumbs

Put the carrots in some lightly slated boiling water and cook for 5 minutes. Drain the carrots. Puree the carrots with a blender or by putting them through a sieve.

Put the rice in a pan of water and bring to the boil. Cook on a low heat for 12 minutes - until cooked. Drain the rice.

Put the carrot puree in a bowl and add the milk, egg, cream and some salt, nutmeg and pepper. Mix in the rice.

Put the mix in a greased baking dish. Put some breadcrumbs on top. Cook in a preheated oven at 200C/392F for 50 minutes.

Serve with meat.

Mushrooms in Cream

Ingredients

900g/2 lb of mushrooms cut into quarters
1 chopped onion
2 tablespoons of vegetable stock
240ml/1 cup of double/heavy cream
butter
salt
pepper

Cook the onions in some butter in a pan for 6 minutes. Add the mushrooms and cook for 8 minutes.

Add the vegetable stock, cream and some salt and pepper.

Bring to the boil then cook on a low heat for 10 minutes.

Beetroot Sauce

Ingredients

5 washed beetroot
2 tablespoons of sour cream
1 tablespoon of apple cider vinegar
salt
pepper

Put the beetroot in a pot of boiling water. Add some salt. Boil the beetroot for 30 minutes - until cooked.

Peel the beetroot and chop finely.

Put the beetroot in a saucepan with the sour cream, vinegar and some salt and pepper. Cook on a moderate heat for 10 minutes stirring several times.

Serve with meat.

Potato Casserole

Ingredients

2.2 lb/1 kg of potatoes
40g/1.4 oz of flour
480ml/2 cups of warm milk
45g/1.6 oz of melted butter
1 teaspoon of salt
1 teaspoon of nutmeg
1 tablespoon of syrup

Peel the potatoes. Place in boiling and cook on a low heat for 10 minutes- until cooked.

Drain the potatoes. Mash the potatoes, then place in a warm spot for 3 hours.

Mix the potatoes with the milk and butter. Add the nutmeg and milk and mix. Add half the syrup and mix.

Put the potatoes mix into an oven dish - fill half way. Drizzle the rest of the syrup on top. Bake in a preheated oven at 150C/302F for 1 and a half hours.

Mushrooms and Buckwheat

Ingredients

226g/8 oz of chopped mushrooms
120g/1 cup of buckwheat
1 chopped onion
butter
1 egg
salt

Mix the egg and buckwheat in a bowl. Put in a pan and cook on a moderate heat for 7 minutes.

Add 500ml/2 cups of boiling water, 4 tablespoons of butter and some salt. Cover and cook on a low heat for 25 minutes - stirring occasionally.

In another pan fry the onions in some butter for 5 minutes. Add the mudrooms and some more butter and cook for 8 minutes.

Mix the mushrooms and onion with the buckwheat.

Finnish Food Facts

Finnish food is quite expensive compared to other European nations. Before Finland joined the European Union in 1995 food was even more expensive with food imports being taxed or banned so they would not compete with Finnish food.

The Finns are said to prefer unsweetened food.

Wild berries such as lingonberries and raspberries are very popular. They are freely available in the many Finnish forests.

Finland has many lakes and rivers and is situated on the Baltic Sea. As a result fish is a very popular dish.

Finnish forests are full of mushrooms and mushrooms are a big part of Finnish cuisine. Finns enjoy mushroom hunting. A popular Finnish mushroom is chanterelle.

Coffee is a popular drink in Finland. Finland has the highest per capita consumption of coffee in the world - 12 kg/26lb per person annually.

Pea Soup

Ingredients

350g/12 oz of dried green peas
1 ham hock
1 onion
cloves
1 chopped carrot
1 teaspoon of dried marjoram
salt
pepper

Put the peas in a bowl of cold water and leave for 12 hours.

Drain the peas and rinse.

Stick cloves in the onion. Put the peas, ham, onion, carrot and marjoram in the pot with some salt and pepper and 1.6 litres/7 cups of water. Boil, then cover and cook on a low heat for 2 hours stirring occasionally.

Take out the ham, take off the meat from the bone and chop and return to the soup.

Mushroom Omlette

Ingredients

370g/13 oz of mushrooms - such as chanterelles
2 onions
6 eggs
500ml/2 cups of milk
100g/3.5 oz of wholewheat/wholemeal flour
thyme
white pepper
salt
butter
grated cheese

Mix the flour and milk in a bowl. Beat the eggs in another bowl, then add them to the flour mix. Add a little salt and pepper.

Line a baking dish with grease proof paper. Pour in the eg mix. Bake in a preheated oven at 200C/392F for 10 minutes until browned. Put the omlette on another piece of paper upside down. Remove the paper on top.

Fry the mushrooms and onions in oil for 6 minutes. Add some salt and pepper and some thyme. Spread the mushroom mix on the omlette. Roll up he omlette and remove the paper. Put back in the baking dish, sprinkle with cheese and cook for another 5 minutes.

Rutabaga Casserole

Ingredients

2 peeled and chopped rutabagas/swedes
30g/1.5 oz of dried breadcrumbs
60ml/1 quarter of a cup of heavy/whipping cream
1 teaspoon of salt
1 teaspoon of nutmeg
2 beaten eggs
3 tablespoons of butter

Put the rutabaga in a pan of cold water. Add the salt then bring to the boil. Cook on a low heat for 20 minutes. Drain the rutabaga, then put them in a sieve over a glass bowl. Push the rutabaga into the sieve using a wooden spoon.

Put the cream and breadcrumbs in a bowl and leave for 5 minutes. Add the nutmeg and eggs and mix. Add the rutabaga and mix well.

Put the rutabaga in a baking dish. Add the butter in pieces over the top. Cook in a preheated oven at 176C/350F for 1 hour.

Spinach Pancakes

Ingredients

160g/5.6 oz of chopped spinach
510ml/1 pint of milk
210g/7.4 oz of flour
2 eggs
salt
pepper
1 teaspoon of sugar
oil

Put the eggs, milk and sugar in a bowl with some salt and pepper. Mix. Add the flour and whisk to make a batter. Add the spinach and a tablespoon of oil and mix.

Heat up some oil in a pan. Spoon the batter in the pan, spread out to make a pancake and fry for 3 minutes on each side.

Fish Soup

Ingredients

2 trout boned fillets (keep skin on)
3 peeled potatoes chopped in half
50g /1.7 oz of celery
3 chopped spring onions/scallions
55g/a quarter of a cup of butter
430ml/1 pint of milk
3 tablespoons of flour
2 bay leaves
spring of thyme
parsley
salt
pepper

Put the potatoes in a pan of boiling water then simmer for 10 minutes. Take the potatoes out and keep the water.

Put the fish in the pan with the bayleaves. Cook on a low heat for 15 minutes. Remove bay leaves. Put the fish on a plate. Put the water in another pan.

Put the butter and scallions, celery and some salt and pepper and the sprig of thyme. Cook for 5 minutes. Add the flour and mix in. Add the water from the other pan. Add the milk. Cook on a low heat for 15 minutes. After 6 minutes add the flaked fish and potatoes. Add some fresh parsley before serving

Pike Gratin

Ingredients

1 pike
150ml /5 fl oz of sour cream
1 chopped onion
1 chopped anchovy fillet
70g/2.4 oz of grated Swiss cheese
salt
pepper

Add some salt and pepper to the pike. Put on a baking tray greased with oil.

Put the anchovy, onion and sour cream in a bowl. Put 2 thirds of this mix on the fish. Bake in a preheated oven at 175C/350F for 40 minutes.

Add the rest of the sour cream mix and the cheese and cook for another 20 minutes.

Liver Casserole

Karelian Stew

Fish Soup

Spinach Pancake

Salmon Roulade

Ingredients

300g/10 oz of sliced smoked salmon
110g/3.8 oz of salmon roe
100ml/3.4 fl oz of sour cream
80ml/2.7 fl oz of whipped cream
60g/2.11 oz of quark cheese
black pepper
1 teaspoon of lemon zest
3 gelatine sheets
fresh dill

Mix the sour cream and quark. Add the pepper.

Put the gelatine in some cold water for 12 minutes, squeeze the
water out of them, then put them in a bowl with 2 tablespoons
of hot water to dissolve. After the gelatine has cooled add to
the cream and cheese mix and stir. Mix in the whipped cream
and salmon roe.

Put the slices separately on a piece of plastic wrap. Spread the
mix on top. Put in the refrigerator for 1 hour. Top with fresh
dill, then roll up the salmon. Put in the refrigerator for 10
hours. Cut into slices.

Shrimp and Egg

Ingredients

slices of white bread with crusts cut off
sliced hard boiled eggs
lettuce
cooked shrimp
mayonnaise
dill
lemon slices
lemon juice
butter

Mix some dill, lemon juice and mayonnaise.

Butter a slice of bread. Put lettuce and egg slices on the bread. Top with mayonnaise and then shrimp. Put some dill and a lemon slice on top.

Fried Herring

Ingredients

herring fillets cut into two long pieces
fresh dill
salt
pepper
rye flour
butter

Coat the salmon in flour salt and pepper. Add some dill to the top of one fillet piece. Put the other piece on top.

Fry in butter for 5 minutes each side.

Finnish Food Facts

A traditional Finnish breakfast is open sandwiches made up of cheese and cold cuts of meat, yogurt and cereal, or porridge with fruit or jam.

Bizarrely in 2005 Italian Prime Minister Silvio Berlusconi and French President Jacques Chirac criticised Finnish food. Chirac said Britain is the country with the worst food."But many famous chefs defended Finnish food and its fresh produce.

Milk plays a big part in the Finnish diet with a variety of fermented milk products. Finns say their cows produce the best milk in Europe.

Potatoes were introduced to Finland in the 18th Century and like many other countries are a staple part of the diet.

There are regional specialties in Finland. For example reindeer from Lapland is enjoyed throughout Finland.

Boiled Fish

Ingredients

900g/2 lb chopped fish fillets
1 chopped carrot
1 chopped onion
225g/1 cup of tomato puree/paste
6 chopped potatoes
butter
salt
pepper
dill

Put the carrot, potato and onion in a pan with some butter and cook for 8 minutes.

Add the fish, tomato and some salt pepper and dill. Cover with boiling water, bring to the boil then cook on a low heat for 8 minutes.

Salmon with Raspberry

Ingredients

salmon fillets
raspberry jam
2 crushed juniper berries
salt
pepper

Mix the jam with the juniper and some salt and pepper.

Put the salmon on a baking sheet. Spread on some of the jam glaze. Cook in a preheated oven at 232C/450F for 8 minutes.

Turn over the salmon. Brush the salmon with more raspberry glaze. Cook for 4 minutes.

Blueberry Gravlax

Ingredients

1 boneless salmon fillet
150g/5.3 oz of blueberries
300g/1 cup of salt
300g/1 cup of sugar
fresh dill

Mix the sugar and salt. Put the salmon on a piece of
parchment paper. Put half of the salt/sugar mix on top.

Put some dill in a baking dish. Put the salmon salt/sugar side
down in the dish. Put the rest of the salt/sugar mix on top.
Mash the blueberries a little in a bowl. Put on top of the fish.
Put some more dill on top. Cover the baking tray with plastic
wrap and place in the refrigerator for 24 hours.

Turn the fish over, cover the tray again with plastic wrap and
refrigerate for 2 days.

Serve sliced.

Fish Pie

Ingredients

450g/1 lb of whole fish gutted, descaled with head removed
450g/1 lb of sliced pork
240g/2 cups of rye flour
120g/1 cup of wholemeal/wholewheat flour
30g/1 oz of dry yeast
salt

Mix the rye and wholewheat flour. Mix the yeast with two cups of water. Mix the yeast mix and flour in a bowl and make a dough.

Roll out the dough into a circle shape. Put half the pork on the dough, followed by the fish and some salt, then finish with the rest of the fish. Fold the dough over to encase the filling. Put on a baking sheet and leave for 1 hour.

Put in a preheated oven at 204C/400F and cook for 40 minutes, then reduce to 121C/250F and bake for 4 hours.

Salmon Roe Sauce

Ingredients

110ml/half a cup of sour cream
100g/3.5 oz of salmon roe
4 tablespoons of chopped dill
4 tablespoons of chopped chives
pepper
salt

Mix the ingredients in a bowl.

Serve with fish.

Prawn Toast

Ingredients

toasted bread
cooked prawns
sliced boiled egg
lettuce
mayonnaise
lemon slices
lemon juice
fresh dill

Put some mayonnaise on a slice of toast. Add a lettuce leaf.
Add some boiled egg slices. Then put some mayonnaise on top.
Put some prawns on top and add some lemon juice.

Garnish with a lemon slice.

Salmon with Cheese

Ingredients

1 kg/2.2 lb salmon fillet
quark cheese
fresh dill
fresh chives
fresh thyme
black pepper
lemon pepper
salt
lemon juice

Coat the fish in some salt, pepper and lemon pepper.

Cut an opening in the salmon. put the cheese inside. Add some dill, thyme and chives on the cheese. Close the hole using wooden sticks.

Add some lemon juice to the salmon, then cook in a preheated oven at 200C/392F for 25 minutes. Remove the wooden sticks.

Macaroni Casserole

Ingredients

600g/1.3 lb of cooked macaroni
430g/1 lb of minced/ground beef
1 chopped onion
3 eggs
1 teaspoon of curry powder
1 teaspoon of paprika
salt
pepper
1 litre/4 cups of beef stock/broth

Put the onion and beef in a pan and cook for 8 minutes. Add the curry, paprika and some salt and pepper.

Grease a baking dish. Put a layer of macaroni in the pan, followed by a layer of beef. Mix the stock and egg. Pour into the dish.

Cook in the middle of a reheated oven at 200C/392F for 1 hour 10 minutes.

Chicken in Sour Cream

Ingredients

453g/1 lb of sliced chicken
225g/half a lb of chopped gherkins
225g/half a lb of celeriac
225g/half a lb of parsnip
3 onions
2 tablespoons of butter
3 tablespoons of sour cream
2 tablespoons of flour
parsley
dill
pepper

Put the chicken in a pan of water. Bring to the boil then cook
on a low heat for 15 minutes - until cooked.

Put the chicken on a plate.

In a pan fry the onion in some butter for 6 minutes. Add to the
chicken broth pan.

Melt the butter in a pan with the flour and make a paste. Add
this to the stock pan with the celeriac, parsnip, onion and
cucumber. Stir then bring to the boil. Cook on a low heat for
20 minutes - until vegetables are cooked.

Take off the heat and add the chicken slices, sour cream, and
some salt and pepper to the pan and stir.

Potato and Bacon Hash

Ingredients

200g/7 oz of chopped bacon
200g/7 oz of chopped cooked beef or pork
2 chopped onions
700g/1.5 lb of cooked and chopped potatoes
1 cooked and chopped carrot
200g/7 oz of chopped mushrooms
100g/3.5 oz of chopped cooked sausage
2 tablespoons of butter
vegetable oil
salt
pepper

Put the bacon and meat in a pan and cook for 8 minutes.

Add the butter and onions and cook for 6 minutes.

Add the carrots, onions, potatoes and sausage. Cook for 6 minutes.

Add the mushrooms and some salt and pepper cook for 10 minutes until everything is cooked - scraping the bottom and mixing several times until everything is cooked.

Beef With Apples

Ingredients

cooked slices of roast beef
apple slices
2 sliced dill pickles
4 tablespoons o butter
4 tablespoons of flour
720ml/3 cups of beef stock/broth
2 tablespoons of lemon juice
3 teaspoons of sugar
salt

Put the butter in a pan and melt. Add the flour and some salt and mix with the flour to make a paste. Add the stock and mix and bring to the boil.

Add the apples, sugar and lemon juice and cook on a low heat for 12 minutes.

Add the beef slices and cook for 5 minutes.

Add the pickle and serve.

Meat Pie

Ingredients

450g/1 lb of minced ground meat
375g/1 and a half cups of cooked rice
1 egg
1 chopped onion
450g/3 and a half cups of wholemeal flour
240g/half a cup of sugar
230ml/1 cup of cream
300ml/1 and a quarter cup of milk
30g/1 oz of dried yeast
113g/4 oz of melted butter
salt
pepper

For the dough, put the milk and butter in a pan. Warm. Put the yeast in a bowl and add the milk mix and stir. Add the flour, salt and sugar and make a dough. Cover the bowl the dough is in and leave for 50 minutes in a warm place.

Put the onion and meat in a pan and cook on a low heat for 12 minutes. Add the rice and cook for another 6 minutes. Add the cream and some salt and pepper.

Roll out the dough and cut into circle shapes. Add the meat filling to the dough circles, then encase the meat filling in the dough. Brush them with beaten egg. Place on a baking tray and cook in a preheated oven at 204C/400F for 25 minutes.

Cabbage Casserole

Ingredients

160g/5.6 oz of minced/ground beef
half a finely chopped onion
340g/12 oz of finely chopped cabbage
60g/2.11 oz of uncooked rice
60ml/a quarter of a cup of beef stock
1 egg
40ml/1.3 fl oz of milk
grated cheese
black pepper

Put the cabbage, beef, onion beef stock and pepper in a pan. Cook on a low heat for 10 minutes.

Put the rice in another pan of water. Bring to the boil, then cover and cook on a low heat for 10 minutes.

Drain the rice, then add to the cabbage mix.

Put the cabbage mix in an oven dish. Mix the egg and milk and pour over the cabbage.

Put some cheese on top then cook in a preheated oven at 200C/392F for 12 minutes.

Finnish Food Facts

Wild berries are picked for free and frozen.

Finland has the northernmost agriculture in the world.

UNESCO The United Nations Educational, Scientific and Cultural Organization has stated that Finnish water is the best in the world. This contributes to the quality of Finnish produce.

Finland is the second largest exporter of oats in the world.

In the 1917 as part of celebrations for the centenary of Finnish independence rye bread was voted as Finland's national food.

New potatoes are very popular in Finland.

One rather odd food enjoyed in Finland is salmiakki licorice. This is salty licorice flavoured with ammonia chloride!

A popular dish in Finland is a ready made spinach pancake which is very popular for school lunches.

Reindeer with Sea Buckthorn

Ingredients

10 fillets of reindeer or venison
cooked buckwheat
480ml/2 cups of sea blackthorn juice
1 tablespoon of flour
1 tablespoon of butter
salt
pepper

Season the reindeer with salt and pepper. Fry in some oil for 4 minutes on each side. Remove the reindeer.

Put the butter in the pan and melt. Stir in the flour and make a paste. Add the buckthorn and some salt and pepper. Bring to the boil then cook on a low heat for 7 minutes.

Put the reindeer on the buckwheat and pour over the sea blackthorn sauce.

Pork Belly

Ingredients

1 pork belly
1 tablespoon of chopped dill
oil
1 tablespoon of chopped parsley
2 teaspoons of sea salt
2 teaspoons of thyme
1 teaspoon of black pepper

Mix the salt, pepper, thyme, parsley and dill in a bowl. Rub over the pork. Roll up the pork and tie with string. Place in the refrigerator for 12 hours.

Wrap the pork in foil. Put in a preheated oven at 176C/350F for 2 hours. Remove the foil and cook at 300F for 2 hours.

Runeberg Torte

Cinnamon Rolls

Bilberryberry Tart

Rice Tart

Ground Meat Soup

Ingredients

450g/1 lb of ground/minced meat
1 chopped parsnip
1 chopped rutabaga/swede
1 chopped stick of celery
6 peeled and chopped potatoes
1 stock/broth cube
1 tablespoon of dried basil
parsley
salt
pepper

Put the parsnip, rutabaga and celery in a pan. Cover with water and add the stock cube and some salt and pepper. Bring to the boil then cook on a low heat for 10 minutes.

Add the potatoes and cook for another 10 minutes -until the potatoes are cooked.

Put the meat in a pan with some salt and pepper and fry for 10 minutes - until cooked. Put the meat in the soup pan with the basil. Cook on a low heat for 6 minutes. Garnish with parsley.

Black Pudding With Sour Cream

Ingredients

black pudding cut into slices
sour cream
butter

Fry the black pudding on both sides in butter for 7 minutes. Add some sour cream and simmer for 5 minutes.

Serve with lingonberry jam.

Stroganoff

Ingredients

350g/12 oz of beef strips
1 chopped onion
butter
500ml/1 pint of beef stock
1 tablespoon of flour
2 tablespoons of butter
1 tablespoon of tomato puree

Mix the flour and 1 tablespoon of butter in a pan to make a paste. Add the stock and cook for 10 minutes stirring all the time until a sauce is made.

In another pan, fry the onion in some butter for 5 minutes. Set aside.

Fry the beef in butter for 8 minutes.

Put the onion, beef, sauce, tomato puree and some salt and pepper in a baking dish

Beef and Beetroot Steak

Ingredients

450g/1 lb of ground/minced beef
1 chopped onion
50g/1.7 oz of oatmeal
1 tablespoon of flour
110ml/half a cup of cream
1 egg
200g/7 oz of grated beetroot
salt
pepper
oil

Put the oats, flour, onion and cream in a bowl with some salt and pepper. Leave for 10 minutes.

Add the meat, beetroot and egg to the bowl. Mix well. Shape the mix into steak shapes. Put on a baking sheet, put some oil on top and cook in a preheated oven at 200C/392F for 17 minutes.

Stuffed Ham

Ingredients

ham slices
smetana
cottage cheese
1 teaspoon of horseradish
half a teaspoon of sugar
salt

Mix the smetana, cottage cheese, horseradish, sugar and some salt in a bowl.

Put some of the mix on a ham slice and roll up.

Karelian Stew

Ingredients

280g/10 oz of chopped pork
280g/10 oz of chopped beef
280g/10 oz of chopped lamb
2 sliced onions
2 chopped carrots
10 peppercorns
2 chopped bay leaves
salt
pepper
vegetable oil

Cook the meat in some oil for 7 minutes.

Put some the meat in a casserole dish. Add some of the carrots and onions. Add some of the peppercorns, bayleaves and some salt and pepper. Repeat the layers. Cover the mix with water. Put in a preheated oven at 150C/302F for 4 hours.

Meatballs

Ingredients

500g/1.1 lb of minced/ground chicken
500g/1.1 lb of minced/ground beef
1 finely chopped onion
45g/half a cup
12g/half a cup of sour cream
vegetable oil
1 egg
2 teaspoons of salt
1 teaspoon of black pepper

Put the breadcrumbs and cream in a bowl, mix and leave for 10 minutes.

Put the onions in a pan with some vegetable oil and cook for 7 minutes.

Put the onion, breadcrumb mix and the rest of the ingredients in a bowl and mix. Form the mix into balls, then place on a baking tray covered with parchment paper.

Cook in a preheated oven at 200C/400F for 20 minutes - until cooked.

Serve with lingonberry jam and mashed potatoes.

Liver Casserole

Ingredients

500g/1.1 lb of minced/ground liver
80g/2.8 oz of cooked rice
1 egg
2 egg yolks
1 chopped onion
100g/3.5 oz of raisins
200ml/6.7 fl oz of milk
50g/1.7 oz of molasses
butter
1 teaspoon of salt

Put the ingredients in a bowl and mix.

Put the mix in a greased baking dish. Cook in a preheated oven at 160C/320F for 1 and a half hours.

Chicken in Tomato Sauce

Ingredients

7 chicken breasts with the bone taken out
56g/quarter cup of butter
4 tablespoons of flour
240ml/1 cup of cream
120ml/half a cup of tomato passata/crushed tomatoes/puree
salt
pepper

Add some salt and pepper to the chicken. Cook the chicken in some butter on a low heat in a pan for 15 minutes.

Put the chicken in a casserole dish. Cover then cook in a preheated oven at 176C/350F for 50 minutes. Add some butter to the top halfway through baking.

Put the juices from the dish in a saucepan. Add the flour and some salt and pepper and stir. Add the tomato sauce ans cream and cook on a low heat for 8 minutes stirring all the time. Serve the sauce with the chicken.

Finnish Food Facts

Finns are particularly partial to cinnamon buns eaten with coffee.

Hernekeitto - pea soup - is normally served on Thursdays in Finland.

Karelian pasties, an open pasty with a rye crust and filled with a savoury rice mix, are very popular.

Blood or black puddings are popular in Finland served alone with sides such as lingonberry jam or in soups.

It is said that Finnish cuisine favours fresh vegetables over canned or pickled ones.

Wild berries are plentiful and popular in Finland and often served with meat as well as in sweet dishes.

Smoked fish is popular in Finland.

Potato Flat Bread

Ingredients

330g/11 oz of cooked mashed potato
110g/3.8 oz of spelt flour
1 egg
half a teaspoon of salt

Mix the ingredients in a bowl to make a dough. Make into four pieces. Roll out each piece on a floured surface. Stick the end of a fork into the dough slices.

Put in a preheated oven at 330C/428F and cook for 15 minutes.

Semolina Pudding

Ingredients

1 litre/4 cups of milk
125g/4.4 oz of semolina
salt

Put the milk in a pan and bring to the boil. Add the semolina stirring all the time. Cook on a low heat for 15 minutes.

Add some salt. Serve warm with butter and fruit.

Barley Bread

Ingredients

240ml/1 cup of milk
250g/2 cups of barley flour
2 tablespoons of melted butter
4 teaspoons of sugar
2 teaspoons of sugar
salt

Put the ingredients in a bowl and mix to make a batter. Place on a greased round baking dish. Cook in a preheated oven at 260C/500F for 17 minutes.

Serve hot with butter.

Pancakes

Ingredients

240ml/1 cup of buttermilk
2 eggs
120g/1 cup of flour
butter
salt
powdered sugar

Whisk the buttermilk and eggs. Add the butter, flour and a pinch of salt and mix to make a dough.

Melt some butter in a pan. Add some pancake batter and cook for 1 minute on each side.

Dust with powdered sugar before serving.

Bilberry Tart

Ingredients

dough

110g/half a cup of butter
110g/half a cup of sugar
1 egg
110g/1 cup of rye flour
110g/1 cup of white flour
1 teaspoon of baking powder
half a teaspoon of cardamom

filling

360g/12 oz of blueberries/bilberries
250g/1 cup of cream
1 egg
1 teaspoon of vanilla
4 and a half tablespoons of sugar
half a teaspoon of cardamom

For the dough, mix the sugar and butter to make a paste. Add the egg, flour, baking powder and cardamom. Make into a dough.

Spread the dough in a cake tin. Cook for 10 minutes in a preheated oven at 190C/375F.

For the filling, mix the egg, vanilla, sugar, cardamom and sour cream to make a batter.

Put the blueberries in the pie dish on the pastry. Add the filling. Cook for 30 minutes.

Baked Pancake

Ingredients

3 eggs
100g/half a cup of sugar
500ml/2 cups of milk
125g/1 cup of flour
butter
salt

Mix the flour, sugar and some salt in a bowl. Mix in the milk and eggs and make a batter.

Melt some butter in a baking dish. Pour in the batter. Bake in a preheated oven at 230C/450F for 30 minutes.

Cinnamon Rolls

Ingredients

1 and a half tablespoons of yeast
200g/ 7 oz of sugar + 1 teaspoon
1 teaspoon of salt
1 and a half tablespoons of ground cardamom
480ml/2 cups of milk
2 eggs
1 kg/2.2 lb of flour
200g/7 oz of butter

filling

160g/5.6 oz of butter
90g/3.1 oz of sugar
2 tablespoons of ground cinnamon

To make the filling, mix the ingredients in a bowl to make a paste.

Put the yeast, milk and a teaspoon of sugar in a bowl. Leave for 15 minutes.

Add the sugar, 1 of the eggs, salt and cardamom and mix well. Add the flour and make a dough. Knead the dough for 10 minutes. Leave the dough in a bowl covered by a damp tea towel in a warm place for 1 hour.

Make the dough into two rectangular shaped pieces. Spread the filling over the top of the dough. Roll up the dough. Cut into slices and place on a baking tray. Cove with a damp tea towel and leave for 30 minutes.

Brush with beaten egg and dust with sugar. Cook in a

preheated oven at 230C/446F for 15 minutes.

Blueberry Pie

Ingredients

500g/1.1 lb of bilberries or blueberries
shortcrust pastry
160g/5.6 oz of caster/superfine sugar
2 tablespoons of cornflour
3 tablespoons of lemon juice
1 beaten egg
cream

Put the bilberries, sugar, lemon juice and cornflour in a bowl.
Mix then leave for 20 minutes.

Lin a pie dish with pastry. Add the bilberry mix. Put a layer of
pastry on top. Brush the egg over the pastry. Bake in a
preheated oven at 190C/374F for 50 minutes. Serve with
cream.

Runeberg Torte

Ingredients

130g/4.5 oz of melted butter
1 teaspoon of baking powder
100g/3.5 oz of flour
60g/2.11 oz of ground almonds
300g/10 oz of breadcrumbs
1 teaspoon of cardamom
1 egg
110g/3.8 oz of sugar
100ml/3.4 fl oz of cream
100g/3.5 oz of icing/powdered sugar sugar
raspberry liqueur
almond oil
raspberry jam
icing

Mix the flour and baking powder. Add the almonds, cardamom and breadcrumbs. Mix the egg, sugar and cream to make a paste. Add the butter. Add the flour mix and make a dough. Add two drops of almond oil.

Put the dough in cupcake tins or paper containers; half fill the container, put some raspberry jam in. then add the rest. Put some raspberry jam on top. Cook in a preheated oven at 200C/392F for 25 minutes.

Put some raspberry liqueur on the cake, some raspberry jam on top and some icing round the top edge of the cake.

Doughnuts

Ingredients

225g/1 cup of quark cheese
300ml/2.3 cup of water
2 teaspoons of dry yeast
1 teaspoon of salt
100g/half a cup of sugar
1 tablespoon of cardamom
1 egg
500g/4 cups of flour
4 tablespoon of butter

Put the quark and water in a pan and heat until warm.

Put the quark in a bowl and add the yeast. Stir, then add the cardamom, egg, half the flour, salt and sugar. Mix, then add the rest of the flour and butter. Mix to make a dough. Leave for 15 minutes.

Put the dough on a floured surface. Make in sixteen balls. Make a doughnut shape from each ball with a hole in the middle. Place on a baking sheet and leave for 25 minutes.

Heat a pan of oil. Fry the doughnuts for 2 minutes in each side. When they have cooled sprinkle some sugar on them.

Fruit Soup

Ingredients

368g/13 oz of chopped dried fruit - i.e. berries
50g/1 third of a cup of raisins
1 litre/4 and half cups of water
30g/1 third of a cup of sugar
1 teaspoon of cornstarch/cornflour
1 stick of cinnamon

Put the ingredients in a pan. Bring to the boil, then cover and cook on a low heat for 40 minutes. Remove the cinnamon.

Can be served hot or cold.

Rice Tarts

Ingredients

Filling

225g/1 cup of rice - short grained
500ml/2 cups of water
1 litre/4.5 cups of milk
1 egg
1 teaspoon of salt

Pastry

240ml/1 cup of water
1 teaspoon of salt
153g/1 and a half cups of rye flour
140g/1 cup of wheat/wholemeal flour
vegetable oil
salt

Put the rice in a pan of water. Bring to the boil, cover, then simmer for 10 minutes. Add the milk and a pinch of salt. Cook on a low heat for 2 hours. Mix in the egg.

For the pastry, mix the flour, water, and salt in a bowl to make a dough. Add some vegetable oil. Mix.

Make 18 pieces from the dough. Roll out each piece of dough.

Put some of the rice mix in the middle of each piece of dough.

Fold up the sides to enclose the mix - but leave a layer of rice mix showing on top of the dough.

Put the pastries on a baking tray and cook in a preheated oven at 204C/400F for 10 minutes.

Rye Bread

Ingredients

100g /3.5 oz of rye sourdough starter
2 litres/8 and a half cups of warm water
3 kg/6.6 lb of rye flour
1 tablespoon of salt

Mix 400g/14 oz of rye flour with the starter. Mix, cover with a cloth and leave for 1 day.

Add 700g/1.5 lb of flour and the salt to the dough. Leave for 1 day.

Add the rest of the flour and make a dough. Knead the dough on a floured surface for 20 minutes. Put the dough in a covered bowl and leave in a warm place for 1 hour.

Make four round flat shapes from the dough. Place on a baking tray. Cook in a preheated oven at 200C/392F for 45 minutes.

Blueberry and Wild Strawberry Cake

Ingredients

wild strawberries
blueberries/bilberries
whipped cream
honey
1 large egg
60g/2.11 oz of sugar
60g/2.11 oz of flour

Mix the egg, sugar and flour to make a batter. Put on a cake tin at cook in a preheated oven at 175C/347F for 12 minutes - until cooked.

Turn out the cake on a piece of parchment paper. Leave to cool.

Spread whipped cream on the cake. Cover with wild strawberries and blueberries. Drizzle some honey on top.

Rye Pudding

Ingredients

6 litres/25 cups of boiling water
600g/1.3 lb of rye malt molasses
1.4 kg/3 lb of rye flour
3 tablespoons of orange rind
salt

Put the hot water in a pan. At the malt and rye flour. Cover
and leave for 2 hours. Mix well, then add the salt and orange
rind.

Put the mix into a baking dish and cook for 3 hours at
150C./302F. Serve with cream.

Long Drink

Ingredients

8 tablespoons of gin
725ml/3 cups of grapefruit juice
3 tablespoons of lemon juice
1 litre/4 cups of club soda
10 ice cubes

Put the ingredients in a jug and mix.

Blueberry Milk

Ingredients

350g/ of blueberries/bilberries
1 litre/4 cups of milk
4 tablespoons of sugar
15 ice cubes

Put the ingredients in a jug and mix well.

Sima

Ingredients

5 litres/20cups of water
800g/4 cups of sugar
100g/3.5 oz of hops
3 lemons
25g/ 1 oz of dried yeast

Peel and slice the lemon - keep the peel.

Boil the water and add the sliced lemon, sugar, lemon peel and hops. Bring to the boil and boil for 3 minutes.

When the mix has cooled at the yeast. Cover and leave for 1 day.

Strain the mix. Put into bottles. Store in a cool place for 4 days.

Mulled Wine

Ingredients

1 litre/4 cups of wine
240ml/1 cup of port
5 slices of ginger
5 cardamom seeds
1 stick of cinnamon
60ml/a quarter of a cup of orange juice
1 tablespoon of lemon zest
3 tablespoons of lemon juice
60g/2.11 oz of sugar

Put everything but the sugar in a pan. Bring to the boil, add the sugar, take off the heat and stir until the sugar has dissolved.

Serve hot.